THE
PLURAL
OF WATER

THE PLURAL OF WATER

POEMS

BRUCE BOND

LOUISIANA STATE UNIVERSITY PRESS
BATON ROUGE

Published by Louisiana State University Press
lsupress.org

Copyright © 2026 by Bruce Bond
All rights reserved. Except in the case of brief quotations used in articles or reviews, no part of this publication may be reproduced or transmitted in any format or by any means without written permission of Louisiana State University Press.

LSU Press Paperback Original

Designer: Kaelin Chappell Broaddus
Typefaces: Scala Pro, text, Scala Jewel Pro Crystal, display

Cover illustration: *Corridor at Dawn*, by Renato Muccillo.
Reproduced courtesy of the artist.

The author would like to thank the editors at the following magazines in which some of these poems previously appeared: *Alaska Quarterly Review, Blackbird, Gettysburg Review, Image, Interim, Narrative, New American Writing, Pedestal, Plume, Poetry Northwest, Terrain, Volt,* and *Verse Daily*.

Library of Congress Cataloging-in-Publication Data

Names: Bond, Bruce, 1954–, author.
Title: The plural of water : poems / Bruce Bond.
Description: Baton Rouge : Louisiana State University Press, 2026.
Identifiers: LCCN 2025045772 (print) | LCCN 2025045773 (ebook) | ISBN 978-0-8071-8616-9 (paperback) | ISBN 978-0-8071-8680-0 (pdf) | ISBN 978-0-8071-8679-4 (epub)
Subjects: LCGFT: Poetry
Classification: LCC PS3552.O5943 P63 2026 (print) | LCC PS3552.O5943 (ebook) | DDC 811/.54—dc23/eng/20251124
LC record available at https://lccn.loc.gov/2025045772
LC ebook record available at https://lccn.loc.gov/2025045773

CONTENTS

WINTER'S APPRENTICE

I. – 3   II. – 15   III. – 25
IV. – 37   V. – 47

THE BLUE MARBLE

I. – 61   II. – 73   III. – 83
IV. – 95   V. – 107

THE PLURAL OF WATER

I. – 119   II. – 129   III. – 139
IV. – 149   V. – 157

Notes – 167

WINTER'S APPRENTICE

Snow is so sensitive to temperature that in borderline intervals it is a matter of just one degree Celsius that causes different shapes to fall from the sky.

— VÁCLAV CÍLEK

I.

Always a note of April in a lily of snow
        laid across the eyes of effigies come dawn.

Call it blindness, foresight, the nature of departure.
    The deeper the blizzard
    the more I see it in the meadows to come.
    I see the boy who held me suspended by my hair
    as another beat me to a deeper color.
    And I refused my dinner. I told no one,
    I tell you. I told myself,
            somewhere out there,

the hidden and abused hold me in contempt.
    Me, I thought, though it was not me.

Confession can feel a little helplessly important.
I was a stranger.

Like the snow that falls one day in April
    to the meadows of a deeper color.

A beaten child will wear in time a newly beaten face.

    It will ask, *do you forgive yourself,*
        and mean, *do you forgive the others.*
            And yes, I say, I do.

    A surge of air will rise into the body of the older boy
        who takes me to his basement.
    He takes my child face.
        He will tell me to undo my buckle,
            and his, to close my mouth.

The world will crumple into small and smaller pieces,
turpentine, rags,
        the caged blue of the furnace fire,
a sway of hammers on their hooks.

The wind against the walls upstairs
        will be my distraction,
        and so, in later years, my bridge.
My witness,
        no sooner there than torn away.

I was a dangerous child
        and blew a neighbor's mailbox to splinters.
        It was beautiful,
                a cottage with adorable windows, real glass,
                a gable, a flag.

Hell, I thought,
he was rich,
and his dogs gnashed the air at the gate.

I struck the way one billiard strikes another,
or a child,
        or if the child refuses, a dream.
The explosion of a small and intricate thing
taught us,
        a body in motion stays in motion.
It said, where designs are broken
                we see the proof of a designer.

And then, the gate began to open.
                It was huge, steel, automatic.
Dogs leapt at the fence and exposed their sex.

                One portion of attention is a wound.

The spirit of revenge is a rage against time,
        wrote Hannah Arendt,
              who later said of Eichmann,
let him hang,
            and can you blame her.

How much intolerance will you tolerate,
        I ask my class, and I have no answer.

Only question, reason, blizzard, cold,
        the pale provocation of talk
        and ashes
              flown across a room.

Just how much are you willing to forgive,
        and we count the five million reasons why
        and not.
        And because each is singular,

        we need time.
        We need someone to build a fire,
        someone to count, one,
                one, as daylight falls

                to pieces, and the snow.

Long ago, I was forgiven,
        again and again, and I go back there,
        when I am bitter,
        to the grace no one deserves.
        Or not.

        I do not know when forgiveness from God
        took precedence over the human kind.
        I apologize,
        I say to a stranger,
        and I get what no one deserves
                or not. I wound and wound.

        If forgiveness were forgetting,
        there is nothing to forgive.
        A field in winter does not forget.
        It goes numb
        beneath the television light
                of clouds that flicker
        long after the graves have closed their eyes.

            If memory were perfect,
                      who would know.

The isolation of the criminal,
    whose cabin lies deep in the woods,
    becomes, in time,
        the better reason to be alone.

    Untouched, the ache beneath the ashes,
    the thrill of the possible
        in an explosive device.
    The kind that makes a statement,
        like *technology is lonely*.
    Or *are you looking at me*.
    The paranoid with his logic
        wears it like a pair of eyes
    to shield the eyes
        that have grown tender.

    Everything happens for a reason,
        says the sentimental
    terror that goes unspoken.
    Are you looking at me,
        replies the undisclosed device.

We are going to need a transfusion of blood and medicine
         for the processional of souls mourned

   in public spaces, windows shattered,
   children dropped from an enormous distance.

   We are going to need to kill the rumor
   nothing happened, and still the rumor rises,
   walks, steps lightly over the dead.

   The living in their skins
   lay down their guns on the evidence table.

   If it were my son,
   I would want someone to testify.

   The world is too much with us
                   and never enough.

   I would want them to hold
   a bullet as they would a match
   in winter,
                  because there is only one.

I grace myself with my own performance.
I wear the shirt of my own gold hair.
I am sorry, I say. *So sorry,*
              say the German children on TV.

They could be talking to my other mother,
a Jew, who smoked,
and when she talked, the soot came pouring out.

Berlin, she said, Better off
broken, and a trace of smoke
                      windowed her eyes.
Suffering has luster, if not fire, although it is neither.
Only suffering.

Not the story we tell, the silence after.
It cannot grace itself with its own performance.

It is not power. Not the suffering of another.
Smoke pours out
            a face that has no face. No hair.

Virtue is haunted
        as hallways are and idols, dolls,
    nights that listen for the step that never comes
but leaves us as we fall.

And all this time I thought empathy was knowing
    how my mother felt,

    but her broken spine taught me, no.
    Virtue is haunted, it said.

When she died, I hardly slept.
    It was no virtue
        to lie awake and listen.

    Grief was the monster in the hall,
        although I never heard him.

        If he left, I never felt him leave.
        If I knew,
            I never knew.

I sleep a little deeper in the winds of late December.

    Trees bend into the shapes of rivers,
            flower eaters, runaways in crisis,
    the mist of the weather-eaten hill
            on its pilgrimage back to sea.

    Just why the rain brings such comfort,
    I cannot say.
    Why we step into the shreds
                of winter garments.
    Have the winds come
            to clarify the garden.

The snow to fill the letters carved in stone.

    When night arrives,
    the stones turn into one great stone.

    If you get singular enough,
            the name ends. Winter begins.

II.

In television light, I cast no shadow.
               I will spare you my story.
   My story is this.
   In Charlottesville,

   I watched a car thrust with disjointed horror
in reverse.
Going back gave the act intention,
                     obstacle, blood,
    a fist against the pulpit.
I look again,
         and still the driver has no face.

My story is this.

If I could enter him, I would have none too.
If I could go back
         and enter the body of the victim.
    If I could look my killer in the eye.

The eye in the eye will tell you.
  A serial killer kills himself.
  Power is always a little suicidal,
  absolute power absolutely.
  When the knife comes out,
      it's personal,
  when it sends a face into the face
  and melts to nothing like a pill.
  To every pill, a symptom,
  to every symptom, pills.
  We could be talking medication
  for a fear of medications.
      Every killer knows.
  Repeat a thing enough, people
     will believe it.
  Repeat it more,
      they lose interest.
  But a mirror does not repeat a face.
  It gets older.
  Go ahead, says the eye in the eye.
    Go on and take it.
      It's yours.

The dead do not remember,
        though they return in the green
    fluorescence of the beetle
      and bronze effigies that do.
Once we feared gods of lightning,
earthquake, plague,
        the chirp of a death-cart at our door.
Now the eye
in the iris
          pulsing with its cursor.
              Nothing more.
Our weapons are just that beautiful,
our pills that strong,
the archetypes of extinction
                  that small-
    boned and personal,
to each the intimacy
of a cry-filled year they will not,
            cannot remember.
Nothing so close
it blurs to no one thing
            falling out of the sky.

I took the figures in the photograph for bones,
    until I looked a little closer.
    (Is it better to look
    or not look. A mother will ask.)
    Bodies pressed against a ledger
    of wire,
    trapped in a library silence
        that eats history with its eyes.

If only I had a picture of the whole occasion,
the gear, the tumbler, the trigger, the mind,
    I might feel less
    the voyeur of another's suffering.

(Is it better to be afraid.)

    If I looked closer
    to see in the gaze of each survivor
    the clasp of the chamber,
    the bladed shutter,
    the million severed threads of light.

Every crisis is a crisis of the eye.
>*The eye,* replied the dark enclosure. After all,
People kill for *ideas*. From the word
idein, to see. If you look hard
enough, things start looking back.
I call it *light* because I have no words.
Every lonely thinker knows,
ideas would be people if they could.
They are that lonely and afraid.
They say people kill for no reason,
but ideas come from somewhere.
From ideas, for instance.
But more than that, from nothing,
which is the weight of an idea.
A terror at first, at times a comfort
with a portrait of a terror inside.
A bit of nothing in all things now.
Where would we be without it.
The bone in the face
                        across the table,
the socket
where the world ends, light begins.

      Why so personal, I prayed.
Is the virtue of the wound
             what it summons,
the caution what it leaves behind.
Make no mistake.
           It feels good to be small
beneath a glass parade of martyrs
whose lesions bleed sunlight as it passes.
He loves us all
felt human, and not,
but who was I.
I was just getting started
    and took my Sundays to the movies,
        where those I love have faces—
   the singing teapot, child spoon—
I wanted to live
     where I was not, and did,
unaware
a part of the personal was elsewhere,
always,
lonely and scared, like a nation of tribes.

If the deeper rule of nature is grace,
    why not let everyone in,
    and my friend replied,
A permissive father is not a loving one.
So why not floor the clouds
in an iron grate to lay bare
the plumbing, the wretched
cloaked in blisters and ash.
Oddly we agreed:
dread and self-loathing
ask a lot of questions.
Was heaven the lie I told my mother
or an accidental truth.
Which is the greater mercy.
Either way, a story
without a clear beginning or end
or none we notice as it passes.
When my mother passed,
    her eyes remained open.
    Still at first,
and then they started to tremor,
    ever so slightly,
        to run their tiny motors on the fumes.

When you see on a flag a mandala,
                        in red and black,
fixed to its canvas with a single star,
you are looking at a savior on fire,
a panopticon tower,
                a Cyclops, a stalker.

Who has not felt a little powerless,
      bound by that
           to the unknown center
                    between us,
      like the nameless
           in a mass grave.
They who bear a nation's name.

I knew a man who beat his child
like the steel
of a swordsmith.
    No more, said the boy.
    Dear God, no more.
    And the flag
           turned back to winter.

III.

My wife, a singer
    (whose cochlea have lost the hairs
    that sharpen the corners
    of words)
    picks out in the passing radio
    the precise pitches
        of an imagined husband.

For that, I am thankful, if not a little amazed.

If the house of memory is made of light,
it takes
    a clock,
    a cadence, an unraveling coil
    to walk us, room to room.
    It takes a pacemaker
    with a tiny hammer
        to make us old
        and small.
        It takes a soul
        out there to hear,
at the end of the hall,
        the reason why
        I listen.

One portion of music is the clarity of rest:
         a dog, a horn,
         the whimper of swing sets
         in a neighbor garden,
         the thump of doors
         we call *the world,*
         never *one* world,
         but broken, sanctioned,
         called.
         The spaces in the song will tell you.

One portion of winter is April always.

         Before we named a door
         the door,
                  we heard it open.

         We heard a moan,
         before the name went in.

         Before it told us, we have heard.

Those who weep to music cannot tell you why.
      Everything and nothing,
          as if there were a form for that,
an anthem for a procession
      of souls. One day a string
      quartet
holds your home to its ear and rattles,
      as if sound were an explanation,
and form the recursive madness
      of our query.
            To those who weep
for joy, I say, it is not joy.
It is rapture.
      A bit of everything and nothing.
And the flame that is the path between.

What song would not return the lost
                who are no less missing,
    no less the whisper *enough*,
            or *more*, or *tell me*,
      are you there.
Are you,
        I ask the friend
who dies each night
        and walks in bone-white paradise
        alone.
In one hand a flashlight,
            in the other a bottle of wine.
I want to say dissonance resolved,
            but silence too has problems.
Once he left
        a box of herbs on my doorstep
to help me sleep.
I thought of that as I chanted,
            Are you there.
I thought of him, as I slept,
            and the words poured out.

I saw each rallentando as the path
                             of the arrow
                deciding to come down.
I saw the face that falls
beneath each face,
the *it* we say, when we say, *it rains.*

I heard a little music in the metaphysics
     of rain.
     It is time,
     I thought, as music filled the chapel.

The deeper the spell
     the more it stings as it whispers,

                You are not alone.

Every dissonance takes two as one
        we hear long before we know it,
    choose it,
or, in the style of fathers long ago,
exclude.
The song a prelude to the understanding
    that comes later,
    as love comes
           to the dissonance of two,
    or one who loves
           to a cold and starless room.
    Tonight,
    leaves
        walk the earth like tiny flames,
somewhere out there, where the world begins.

It comes from here, Janis Joplin said,
        pointing at her gut. Then she laughed,
              not because it was funny,
just something a body does,
        because it is alone.
It knows,
you can hear a little suffering
        in the higher registers of laughter.

She laughed a lot
at her high school reunion,
    holding a bottle in one hand,
            confiding in the camera.

It comes from here,
    she said, and pointed
        at the neglected child there,
the one
who hears what a singer hears
            as unheard still.

Given the ringing in my head,
    I tried to walk a little faster,
                leaving it behind.
If I am short, I am sorry.
Last night a rustle of trees,
but when I looked,
                the branches were bare.
My little misery, my unwanted guest,
are you any less.
My something from nothing,
        look at all you taught me.
The two of us bound
as masters are to those who serve them,
feed them, press their laundry,
                sharpen their knives.

Today as I chanted in my head,
            I walked with one eye open,
    I sent a wave of ink, side to side,
              across the damaged cells.

I think it's working. Not sure.
So I will walk the same cold
tomorrow, same street cleared
of traffic by the plague,
the city lonely as a trainset.

I will snip the light into a montage
of disasters,
nightsticks, breathing machines,
            the refrigerated truck,
a plume of exhaust
by the hospital morgue.

I will walk into a field of snow
           and never touch the ground.

We take what we are given,
         the way a song takes air and gives it back.

Where the breathing goes remains unclear,
but music gives the breathing a pair of sails.

It walks a churchyard
full of strangers who feel an affinity
as strange.
I have walked my shadow
              as long as I remember.
Every dawn a monster, every noon a nail.
The older faces
     of your lovers will surprise you.
              Like snow in June.
   Fall was a child the day paradise was born.

IV.

When I was small, my mother kissed my wounds,
    if they were small,
             tiny in their fractal magic.
The greater injuries needed time
which kisses no one,
          although it watches.
Turn away,
          and time is there,
          closing every child's
          lesion with its eyes.

One portion of vigilance is helplessness.

    The other the nervous mercy of the new.

Why is *pain* our word for the loneliness of experience.
    Why not *experience*.
    Why not *pain* as the motel
            room with no one else around.
    Why not *room*.
    Why not the space of a room long after we have left.
    I have seen the images
            of the others in *room*.
    I talk aloud to the ones that are empty.
    I am here, here, my mother said,
    over and over,
    to find her answer
            in the failure of a name.

Today a student came to me,
      a shiver in her voice and hands,
and asked for time away
      from the others, and yes, of course.
The silence around words felt merciful,
      brittle, as calm
as a house when the power goes,
the freezer leaks,
      the meat parcels begin to bleed.
I learned from mother
      to say *I'm sorry* for the world.
She leaned in, cleaning the broken part,
      binding it in cotton.
When my student spoke,
      I said sorry for something
            I am not meant to see.
The violence of seeing followed us,
      bound us.
      So yes,
            take time, space,
      whatever you need,
            as if they were mine to give.

When I was young, I was a face
        in a lover's eye, a figure in a spoon,
   a pattern that echoed
            in small and smaller versions.

        As if forever were a thing
        we see
without knowing we have seen it.

My car glided from under the bridge,
and I said I wished I met her later in life.

She hooked her blouse, fixed her hair,
confessed she did not understand.
                I did not either.

    A part of me was a step ahead,
        broken off from where I was.
    My other part in a car with her,
       a bright black rain
            across the road
       I barely knew was there.

I hurt, I hurt, my mother hollered to the lobby,
    hand raised to hail the singer
        come to cheer the ladies at the home.
He was a ridiculous blessing
    in a style
        of glad that belies a note of anger.
Huge grin, polyester collar,
        tiny crappy karaoke machine,
but he understood something
I did not
    about the mercy of the artificial.
I hurt, my mother shouted,
    and he waved back, mid-song, oblivious
    or pretending.
No matter. It was a group song after all.
    He came to sing.
The whole damn world came down a flight to sing.

The wind on my face takes the shape of a face.
A ripple across the fathom,
                      no sooner there than torn away.

And I know the deeper wound will one day surface.
Music will flay a layer, flay another.

                My wounds are not original.
      They are personal.
    Music tells me.
The rain on the roof turns, as it falls,
                    into a box of glass
I should be water now,
but a face keeps emerging.

      My friend's life had a shape, an end.
                I took it into hiding.
      I hoarded. I slept.
            I called his memory *his*.

In his final days,
       he sought an end to the untouched life.
               He sought the untouched life.
So when I found in his closet
          a gag ball and leather straps,
I wondered if it helped,
who wore what, who he was
              when he was there.
Was the heart a drunken starlet
knocking at her own locked door.
Go on and ask.
How much artifice does it take to strip
the art,
to peel a layer
    of helplessness or shame,
        now that you are naked and unreal.

Is there a safe-word we should know,
a script,
a hairpin to pick the vault of last night's wish,
with instrumental pain.

Time does not pass
                precisely.
Only experience as it falls
into faces we find *beautiful*,
aka the fire
you love that eats the candle.
A portion of attention
      is
    what we call it
        after it is gone.
    It is December,
and a woman sleeps in a chair
beneath a blanket.
In her lap, tomorrow's news.
If this is heaven,
          I have seen it.
I have felt it shiver through the trees
    on a night
    that has no face
        but hers.

V.

Am I a child to be scared of nothing,
                        unspecific as politics,
                        kindness even.
When bones become unspecific,
they begin the darker
                        leg of the journey.
They become a field in winter.
                        A peace comes over them.
The sun inside Earth welters and fades.
                When a mother grows specific,
she gives to each a name:
cup, chair, mother.
When she leaves, she takes them with her.

Grief is a field like this.

Sun falls to earth in perfect silence,
                as if the light were nothing. Like the snow.

When an ocean sobs,
          it mourns a lot of no one.
A little of all.
Any wonder it cures the sleepless.
When I can't sleep, I drop anchor
beneath the face on the water,
and the light across the surface flowers.
I pierce the glass of a computer
with its montage of houses
where I live.
         Sometimes I write a stranger
    with my name
        and ask about the ocean.
    Is it finished grieving.
I say,
we are going need a new word,
you and I,
         for modern loneliness.

We need the unheard voice
            in any given conversation,
     the one who hesitates,
   yes, but,
to keep our hunger honest and alive.
And while we're at it,
            a new diagnosis
for those who suffer their exclusion,
  if only to fall in love
      with a hand
           in a funny move
    as it scurries into its box.
It kept me safe.
I miss you, hand, will you ever go away.
Are you out there pulsing.
        If I choose you, will you answer.
Will you open the screen
          in the screen and so on,
   just you and the world
              like mirrors.

Where choices go, tragedies follow.
    I call to them as I might a dog
    I sleep with.
    A paw will catch me,
            and I give her a pat on her head.
Good girl, I say.
        I say that a lot for nothing,
           also known as being
           there.
When I talk, she cocks her head
to tilt my voice toward a particular ear.
Misunderstanding has brought us closer.
Each the apprentice, the master of the other.
On my bed at night, I hear her breathing.
I feel her twitch.
She falls asleep so easily.
            Me here breathing in the distance.

          Is the eye in the eye
of the wound called as witness
veiled in these bright obscurities of blood.
Does it see what the starless see,
               what suffering imagines.
Is it wise. Or merely vigilant.
Does it see what knowledge must
               when afflicted and alone.
Do your wounded parts long to survive.
     (What did we expect.)
Are they people now,
    cloisters, cells, communities of trust.
Is the need to recoil itself a skin,
   so when I touch it,
               I feel wounded.

I thought I knew my enemies and friends,
    until the season took them.
    The smallest days were diamonds.

Pain was literal as numbers.
        It consumed my flesh in blisters.
After everything, I tried nothing.

Alan Watts told me I was not my pain.
My pain was on a shelf out there.

But what I found was a box
    with *Pain* written on it.
        An altarpiece, a souvenir.
A portion of attention
is memory.
Always.
        The other a clearing away,
a breath blown through
    the small and smaller embers.

When I was on the bathroom floor
   in seizures,
     I thought of an ocean,
          impersonal as stone
          in its magnificence,
beyond all cruelty and conscience,
I played music in my head.
My song
out there
    like an image on TV.
The voices looked so lonely,
world-less,
clueless,
    far from here with its vertigo
    and linoleum tile.
To give the chords letters
    seemed an intimate estrangement.
    The chords were always elsewhere.
    I cast them back,
        as one who casts a vote
    of conscience
        into the open sea.

Some animals know they are dying
and wander into the ivy in the night.
When I was a child, I found him
shaking in the leaves, beaded in rain.
As if he needed to be alone. Someone did.
Even as I carried him,
                waiting for the sky to clear.

The wind excludes no one.
            You can hear it in your sleep.
You hear what a wind becomes.

The body, two bodies.
            The wind, two winds.
One of which is silent.

Tonight I note in the one the other.

In every sound, the part I call *wind*
    or Father
        or Do not leave.
So when I wake
        I hear more clearly.

The heart beneath my pillow
            and the bedroom floor,
      I hear it in its silent context.
   I hear the snow
as it falls around a house
at night,
    the furlough and drift,
            the closing of a wound.

THE BLUE MARBLE

A fervid utilitarianism has a strangely revolutionary force: in squeezing the world to get every drop of pure good out of it, it leaves the world worthless, and has to throw it away: nothing remains but the immediate good of the spirit, the naked soul longing to be saved.

—GEORGE SANTAYANA

I.

When I was small, I found in the hills a battered car,
    the casualty of a fall, a vandal,
        acid rain that ate the fabric from the wire.

The beauty of decaying things leaded
        the blood of my eyes,
    so I would think of it often, when I was alone,

    the metal of the hood that bore
        the colors of dusk,
    the rust in patterns of the runoff
        that longed to return.

But it never returned. Nothing does.
    A little of nothing in everything.
    A little of each
        in suns that crash
    and shards that are the diamonds of the bees.

Give me proof, said Thomas,
    and he could see a hole in the palm before him,

    and inside the wound a glimpse
        of the valley on the other side,

    what I call, for want of other words, *the world,*
    never *my world,*

    never the earth faith alone imagines.

    This year is the hottest year on record,
    and you can feel it pouring through the hole.

    You can feel the wind that is invisible,
        though we see it in the olive trees,

    what the air moves aside, as if to say,
        Am I not the proof you wanted.

    Am I not the blood.

If pasture scripture, so too the page.
                Every blade drinks a language,

    the way silence drinks a hymn,
    or science the alchemical equipment.

    Responsibility drinks the wonder that opens its eyes.

The year I was sick, I wrote a letter in my sleep.
    I sent it to the moment before.

    I so wanted to reach the place
                my family came to rest.
    When the letter arrived, my eyes had eyes.

Some days earth is such good company,
    I say, *thank you, I missed you,*
    and feel my voice
               vanishing across it,
    as people do
        and stone beneath the carved initial.

The marriage of attention and imagination
        is
          out there, somewhere,
    where science looks at alchemy and whispers,
I too dream of you.

        How odd to be alive.
        Alchemy reminds me.

Just today I was nursing a wound
    and turned into a child.
    The way it shone when I cleansed it.
    It made me
    careful. It made me look again.

    As if the eye were lead,
        and the dusk across the surface, gold.

If one were one
>	with a tree, who would think to ask
>	a tree, the thought of whom is silence.

What branch would lean through the window
>	and whisper.

Plato saw learning as remembering,
which is when knowledge is something
we did not know we knew.
>	If you are lost, you are not alone.

When I am lost, I love to get more lost
where the streets curve
>	in deference to the rivers.
Me here, the planet there,
a gravity between us. It taught me how to run.

And when I ran, I felt a little freer
>	from the pull of it.
I felt the pull.
And when I stumbled, I went numb.
As if my flesh were flesh alone, and earth
>	earth.

I have walked this path in a game called *Death
    for Beginners*,
        tempted as I was to fall.

If I stepped on a fracture, I would scream
softly to myself.
For it was early,
the streets sedated in fog.
The drapes of homes burned dimly,
if at all.

Long ago this place was naked.
        Then the sidewalks came.
                They laid their faces over
the eyes of gods,
where the children pressed their hands.

You can see them still,
beneath the life that fructified the surface.

        Like a superstition of graves.

The uneven path taught me to be careful.
    My body taught me to extend my arms.

Balance, it said, *is a variety of flight.*

Alan Watts taught me. Asymmetry brings relief.
    Like symmetry, I echoed.

    Like music in movies when you fall
    in love with virtue. Or music.
    Or Alan Watts. A conversation
    where the echo of the echo
    curves
        into a tree in a parking lot,
    a joke among mourners, a child's boo.

And everyone laughs because they are lonely.
    A cross above the dresser gleams.
    In accidental light, it glows and darkens.
        In the body
                of the planet, it pulses.
    Breathes.

All is mind, he said,
>   his hand a figure in the field
> that turned into *a garden*
>   where every bird's anonymous.
> Who has not looked for patterns in stone,
> a face that says,
>   *Did you think I forgot.*

> We were all so different then,
> lost in a host
>   of undisclosed relations.
> *You are all alone out there,*
>   he added,
> and Earth dwindled to a marble in the dark.

> Imagine our good fortune,
> cradled in nothing, as all things are.
> The sound of rain
>   running from the rain.

5,400 species of songbird, not to mention song.

5,400 breeds of nothing, the lost
inhalations of song
in the bloodline of the unconceived.

And sometimes a crackle,
and a bird flutters out the mouths of children.

Take of this, my flesh, he said,
and he held up a tiny planet,
so small I thought it was an eye

without a pupil, a transparent ball
    with a sky inside.
And smaller versions of ourselves.

I had a teacher who chanted *holy*
        to bless the drought-worthy weed
        in parking lot
        where runaways can find each other.
Holy the angel-dust
        in the eyes of a thousand windows
to witness all that Moloch gave world.
Holy the forlorn cab,
the fire eater, the tattooed girl
beneath an overpass in a bracelet of fog.
Holy the breath that blushes a mirror
with a note of surprise.
Holy the dawn that dismantles
        the logo on the office of silent affairs.
Holy the alif, the claw,
the dumpster, the epitaph to a library fire,
the kiln that killed an aunt. Holy the ditch
that ate a century, chased it with gasoline,
and woke, blind.
                Holy, my teacher wept,
his body a cup
        on the altar,
        his voice so tender, the cup disappears.

II.

The woman at her microscope closes one eye
    to clarify the other.
    Somewhere down there is the hook
            she hangs her coat on,
    her morning cup of coffee with a face inside.

The butchered rhino in the jungle,
        he too is there,
in a home that is bigger,
        as Earth grows small.

When I was a child, I was selfish.
    An angel watched through a hole in the sky.
    But now the hole is larger,
    and the sun glares through,
    and the weeping of the north has touched
    the Syrian farmer.
    When I open my eyes, half the world remains
    in the weathered refuge
    of a tent
        or craft at sea,
        the throng of untouchables
    like angels on a pin.

Leave it to a science to talk to the dead
        molecular arrangement,
    to wander the wild and christen every genus.
Ever wonder why
the sleepless look at you,
called to see
what wilderness sees,
the ghost machinery that makes a child
        fall in love with science.

I called this one *Lily*, that one *Stone*,
        the other *a lonely a kid with a shovel*.
              I opened the appendix
of a history of the garden, confused by names
        I might have known,

    in a language I read backwards
        toward the more embedded and obscure.

Split this atom, and you find in the center
        a pair of scientists, deep in love.
    Deeper still
    the labor that will, in time, destroy them.
When I think of them, reunited,
    their portrait an x-ray lit from behind,
    I call this light *the instability of nature*.
Soon enough the war will lay its bodies at our door.
    Where to put them,
        I do not know.

Where to set to rest a dangerous knowledge
    save in the vault of knowledge to come.
    We are going to need a new faith,
        the kind you show a child
    the evening of a nuclear crisis,
    when you tell her *don't be a stranger, call,*
        and give her a car,
    and the mist eats her taillight down the road.

I am walking through a kitchen in the desert of Nevada
    where all the kids are plastic,
arms raised in postures of bewildered awe,
heads askance
      to roll a problem
          to the shaded side of mind.
A parody of attentions
              that never blink
    and have no child in them.
No one meets the eye of another,
though they stand
in conversation
where it matters less what you say,
more that you speak a given direction.
They are not alone.
Slip, online, into a bracelet of fire,
reunited with a landscape that never was.
Your radiance will glaze a field
        of glasses in the distance.
And then, applause.
The crackle of a river reaching the sea.
Rest assured.
        You will never be alone.

A lake, touched, is the sky inside.
    A cloud the fish that shatters it to needles.
        A needle, touched,
           wears a crown.
Come evening,
    we lay a dollar in a field-guide,
    enfold the meadow of the pages,
        rub our eyes.
You can tell the age of these hills
by their readiness to crumble.

    A finger, touched, becomes a mirror.
    Once,
my cat growled at her image in the half-lit hall.
    The glass was dead, but in the dark,
           the darker
       figure
           was alive.

Earth's lung is a forest in flames
        that eats air and medicines like children.
Take these, the forest says,
one to cure the daughters of Chernobyl,
another the antigens of the harvested heart,
and there, the root to end all nightmares.
But what I held was nothing,
the way a radio
        tuned to nothing local and clear
holds *no one thing.*
      Which is a word I use for everything.
A word for those who are childless.
The silence of all in the silent one
                who never was.

I had a radioactive friend,
    the son of a radioactive mother
        who cried for no reason
and hid from her children with her face
in her hands.
I never knew what would set him off.
We must have wounded one another
with a readiness to suffer.
Instability is contagious in nature.
    I am sorry, sorry,
    and on it goes.
Everything I know is dark around the edges.

How beautiful the tube of green light
    Marie Curie took to bed,
        something of a comfort
as her blood turned cold.
        A comfort and a friend.

When I first saw Earth
    from a distance,
               an inch above the horizon
    of the moon, I placed it
under a microscope to find a child
below
with a microscope and tiny address.
So too my knee,
    the address of some enormous ghost
who whispers *closer*
as she pulls away.
When I first saw Earth as a marble,
      I was the child
no more.
      I was a child's child
from a fable
where the planet grows small and smaller,
as people do
    on the verge of disappearing
                like a god.

III.

Dear Earth,
    When I think of you, I see you
        in the patio of the New York Deli,
Boulder, Colorado, 1976,
      a cup of coffee, a book
      of *Dream
      Songs*,
      the lifting of your head
      an awakening,
      the closing of your book
      a tune.
      For so long, I saw each friend
      as a figure in a landscape,
      less and less a feature
               of the land.
          When I dream, I am
                every person
                in the dream,
                lives unread
                until they leave us.
      Who is that child with my name,
      digging for all
               I cannot know.

Regret is dread whose tomorrow is forsaken.
    But a friend, never.
    It must be contagious, the desire
        to be here
            and not,
to share blankets, needles, fears that make us
followers.

We could have taken him in, I say,
and the earth below turns back to earth.

When I think of him, I think of earth.

I think of how he hung above it,
    how neighbor children spied his rope
and head
    behind the leaves, above the fence.

Those who float their song an inch from Earth
    no sooner feel the summons to return.

All heaven needs is an inch,
    a breath to lay a loved one in the pasture.

Praise these bells, the chorister sings,
how they come to rest inside a music.

Willows dip their nets a little deeper.
Any wonder the scent of briars lingers
    on our shirts.

Our hands were there all afternoon.
    These little wounds bear witness.

When I am closest to Earth,
    I am
        closest to the lost
            home of song.

When I was wounded and lost my calling,
      I lived not far from a lake
      the city set aside,
      a railway station
      where no one comes or goes.
      How beauty raises the wave
      it mends,
      I do not know.
             Only that a lake
             is more than I ask
             for now.
If kindness is beautiful,
so too the field it writes on.
This park with its shallows,
its needles,
its patch of shade,
could be our villa by the sea.
      Seen as is,
the lake is a city
    the way an arm,
           touched, is the person inside.

When gratitude is final, it sinks and blurs
        into the less particular
        silver.
        It forgets,
        as wishes forget the disbelief
        that made them
        float.
        My father's body was a broken clock
        with a lion on the crest.
        Beautiful, useless,
        timeless.
        I have read the nothing of things
        is
        their non-essential nature.
        But it is more.
        At the end, my father and I sat
        and talked
                a broken English.
            Nothing is always more.

A body leaves the body it was,
        its lust, luster, misdemeanors,
        the deeper colors of the scars,
        and still we call our features
        ours, the way an ocean calls
        its water by a river's name.
        I turn to the photograph and say,
        There I am,
    by the marquee of the Crown Theater
        that later turned into a brothel,
        then an office, then,
        the smell of oceans in the breeze.
        Movies freed us,
        our share in the crisis
        vanquished as the credits rolled
        and the soul fluttered back
        into its cage.
        How little I understood,
        my head full
of nothing
        I recall, thinking
                it would never change.

A child wakes in the dark a mother leaves behind.

    Out of nothing, nothing.
    Out of no one thing, a mother tongue.
    How odd to speak of none
        and wonder
            who in there is listening.

    When did nothing get so serious
        it kept its silence at the party.
    But now and then you hear it
    when laughter dies
        and a grave in air awaits a word.

    Out of mouths of friends, a need
            to be original and so
        remembered and so, again,
      a stranger.
    I too wake in the dark.
        I keep a journal by my bed,
    every ghost forgotten, every word a ghost.

When the time comes
        and a body leaves you
           in a basket of black fabric, take heart.
        There is always more.
        Ever a trace of anger taken for the love
we keep on losing.
A friend drives his shame into a wall,
        and the shame drives on.
If I kneel to read,
        I can put my finger in the letters,
where the stone, however inscribed,
        is stone,
           that fire in the distance,
                the absolution of the flies.

He was the casualty of a mother.
    Calm as a doll, she held his head,
opened his mouth,
stabbed his tongue with a steak knife.
Some unkillable thing
              oddly fought her to survive.
    And now, years later,
to just sit here, look at the sky,
have a burger, and think,
this is good, this is good enough,
how great is that,
pain in a box with *pain* written on it.
And because the moment is good
enough, no one says.
    No angel falls
        through a hole in the tongue.

    The love of place is silence.

If I knew what death is, why would I say so,
    over and over,
             in the anthems of my tribe.
Why wander in tears into paradise
        if only to kiss the ground.
A failure to align binds us like magnets.
Of which the Earth is one,
the word for *Earth* another.
To the ants who raise a silent roar
like a dome of light above a city,
I say,
Today's lesson is in tenacity.
Thoreau taught me.
From the Latin *tenere*.
      And to think I named things to *hold* them,
          but I do not hold them.
    I thank them,
        as if to say goodbye.

IV.

VI

The shadow figure of a shoulder in the water tells you
           night has fallen through.
    A vein-shade as somnolent as marble
lies down across the face.
So what remains swings its gate
both ways.
In and farther in.
When I was a child,
I loved the alchemy,
the parting sea of material nature,
      that said,
         I know, life out there is lonely.
    That was years ago,
               and I stared for hours.
So cold and clear the mirror,
         I could not hear the others.
    I could not hear my name,
so various the water,
          forever letting go.

Long ago, the sea was the road
                souls traveled into life.
   Soul, from the Norse for sea.
                  So say the missing ones
beyond the whitecaps,
               the salt in the wind,
the graves of ships across the ocean floor.
What do we know,
they whisper.
     So light their step,
they leave no trace.
          Only the sea that gave us words.
    Remember.
The core of each is empty and vast.

The stories you have heard are not true,
      I said to a handful of strangers.
            I was talking to a map
archaically imagined,
  a terra incognita whose caption read,
        The truth is never true.
These days online
  you can work wonders with images
of others.
Every year, we grow a little younger,
      the atom bomb a little older,
ever more obscure the island
at the center,
        how the ocean weltered
and closed.
Some would say it mended.
    You could sail right over
        and never know it's there.

Whitman is in the ocean again,
    blessing, *death,* splashing like a child,
    but when the war comes,
    the infinite shrinks to the size a man,
        a leg, a pin
        in the sleeve of an amputee.
Too soon a shipwreck becomes *the sea.*
It tars the feet and hair of bathers,
climbs our streets,
lays a poisoned fish against our plate.
It's with us still,
    what we netted, seasoned, charred,
the smell of rosemary and lemon
        clinging to our aprons like a child.

In a red flag season with cameras on the bluff,
    breakers pound the shore.
    They want what every insomniac wants.
        They want in
            and beat our skeletons to find it.
        However old your hands,
you are older.
You were old the day you almost drowned.
        If you cannot sleep,
        know
        the hole in the ocean floor needs you.
        It needs your sense of betrayal,
        your circle of the underworld,
        the dread
            that is the food of angels.
The mouth that drowned needs your breath.
Thank you, you whisper, as it pulls you through.

When I lay beaten by the ocean.
>	I told myself I deserved it.
Not for what I did but who I was.
I told no one.
I told a stretch of water off the public pier.

Every dream is a good dream,
the horizon said.
>	And then, silence.

Whenever I feel beaten, I go back.
A stranger,
I seek the comforts of the strange.

A reader then.
My face a lantern in the water.
>	And in my pupils, waves.

What was I thinking, says a lapsed romantic
        by a portrait of a wreck at sea.
Who am I to make a mother out of nature,
    he asks,
           and the painting is our answer.
The sacrament tastes more like blood
        to one who knew it once
        as wine.
And lo, the darker view becomes the more
charitable:
sleep's dominion afloat a dreamless tide.
whose solace
bears no gratitude,
           no tragedy or glamor.
    The ocean slides over the lips
      of sleepers
      and doors
           because it does not care.

The chemistry of blood will tell you.
        Life crawled out of an ocean once.
                It carried a sack of brine.
    If the molecules are listening,
            they must be missing home.
        Like a portrait
of a house
      at night, the last light inside a curtain.
I barely knew my home
          until the day I lost it.
I lost my sea the day it overtook the shore.

Once, I looked at the sea so long,
>> I saw kindness as a question.
> Like.
> If power corrupts, why give it to our friends.

> Or.
Is that you, Lord, in waves that are the children of storms.

> Is that your shy fist at the door.

>> *Are you alright, love. Are you there.*

V.

Dear Future, was that you who
              wrote in chalk,
      Play is the work of childhood.
Remember the girl
who could not find her doll.
You told her a story,
     how, somewhere on its journey,
it sent its love.
     You could tell by the hand
on her lips, she held love's silence in.
I need not tell you.
          A doll's life never ends.
When I read the chalk,
    I hear the branches behind me
and above.
I hear the white noise of the leaves.
Or is that you.
       Coming or going.
         As if
            it made a difference.

A bird on the verge of extinction is a child,
                and I follow with my flashlight
    and a book about birds.
    I cannot tell you why,
only that death brings out a more endearing nature.

The garden remembers nothing of course.
      No faint impression on the grass.
A gardener sweeps the flowers that have left us.
      But the garden never does.

In it, a flock without number.
        Fish come blossoming red and gold.
When I am mended, I am two people,
      seer and seen.
               By the mercy of that, a reader.

To each their narrative, their truth,
        his voice as small as Earth from a distance
where the dinosaurs are friends.

I want to say, kindness has courage in it.

But I stay silent, small. I want to say,
we are all held by death, as friendship is,
        and Earth in the darker clarities that burn.

With wonder begins the trepidation.
I want to ask,
when is the wound a blind spot,
when a lens.
        I want to say what the Earth said once.

To see your pain in the darkening grove is dawn.
        To darken there is darkness.

No time to be sentimental about madness
    and therefore repetitious.
    We are readers after all, spared the ache
        of those who have so little imagination
they are one with everything
and thereby all alone.
Five million plus breeds of delusion
swept a people from the face of Europe.
In each, a city with no one in it.
Only cries.
And then a man with a battle-cross on his coat
replies,
    Go back to bed, my little ones.
    It is nothing.
        Believe me, it will soon be gone.

I would like to announce my candidacy
    for commissioner of fire,
      said the fire,
and little blazes cropped up everywhere.
They ate a crowd in Virginia,
                books in Berlin,
    the word *fire* in a small sample study.
They broke into Our Lady of the Light,
and stole the artifacts.
              Given what we lost,
    you would think we knew more
           about our subject.
But we were lonely,
    scared of all the wrong things,
        as children are of clowns,
           Frankensteins of candles.
Suspicion makes a soul susceptible
to pride,
as flames are when they panic,
           when we fall to our knees,
              ear to the planet,
          and blow.

Lights as angels, the days behind us,
        and ahead. Even the night
                your house burned down.
All your neighbors pooled into the street,
strangers in their robes, eyes
lacquered in the light that swelled.
How quick the ascension
                that pleads for refuge.
But it does not leave.
Nothing does.
                No updraft of the cinders.
No mother weeping like a candle
      deep inside the smoke
                    you breathe.

I was riding a bus, late, in the Haight District.

Just me, a driver, and a man, drunk, alone and singing.

I looked at the trees and saw him in the dark reflection.

I was young, afraid of what I did not understand.

    I was ashamed.
                  Who was I to call it sad, the rain.

The song in the dark and the branches passing through.

Then I leaned down,
        my ear the dome of a little chapel,
and the ant said.
*Have you seen the children dousing us
in lighter fluid,*
        texting cruelties to their friends.
What did I know of ant prayer
and remonstration, ant pain.
Alone. I listened. I knelt. Alone.
I put a dollar in a jar
        labeled *every pointless creature.*
In wonder begins responsibility,
                      the ant said,
and together we felt the dome
            of an enormous ear,
            descending overhead.

THE PLURAL OF WATER

To murmur, Yes I remember. What an addition to company that would be. A voice in the first person singular. Murmuring now and then, Yes I remember.

—SAMUEL BECKETT

I.

Before I ever made sense, I made a music.
    I was small
        in a train that huffed
    its brakes,
        and a woman stepped down
    out of the cattle car,
her child beneath the hood of a shawl.
There were others I could not see,
        though I heard the whistle
and the feet that answered
        to a general thunder under way.
I want to say she was singing to the child
        just moments before.
        I hold her in my mind
the way a woman holds a child,
        and I know it is nonsense.
    This singing.
I know the child is unlikely to recall.
    Or if she does,
she can never know just what she knows
    when she weeps for no reason.
For no reason,
    she says, she says again,
    when she smells a train
        on the officer's kiss.

The dry cleaner's dumpster, the luminol, the glove,
    the chill
        of office neon in the night.
Just as a million phones were lighting up at dawn,
    the angel
                of bare essentials arrives.
The body on the embalmer's table turns to silver.
Her name remains as flowers do
                          a while longer.
     It lingers in the paper
        like ice and stars in the morning.
When a river meets a river,
    the name of the smaller one
    dies.
                      But the waters rise.
The flesh remembers.
When darkness falls, one light fades
                to feed the others.

The wound is not an opening in the body.
    It is the body.
               It pulls no door
                to the royal chamber,
    lays bare no true,
                small, and suffering thing.
If passion consumes my flesh,
what is left is flesh
without angel,
                angel without flesh.
No lamp in the dead letter office.
No note scribbled in crayon and blood.
When I was small, I wanted revenge
in night terrors that beat me senseless.
What I suffered turned to water.
But every rainfall it returns.
What did I know
of who I was,
what a bruise becomes,
who takes who when a child is taken.

Survivors of the shooting find solace in numbers.
    They count casualties because precision matters.
    It preserves.
    A woman sees her body still
drenched in blood,
            some of which is hers.
    She asks, why call yourself to remember.
            Every backfire is a gun.
    Must the ending of our suffering be suffering,
            when, over and over, it ends.
    One buries the dead in the body
            the way the number one is buried
in all others, divisible by one.
    The second grief is the dimming of the first,
        one half wounded,
  the other
        children's voices, passing through.

A mother stitches a name into a jacket
    a child will outgrow,
        though the name will follow
another child,
it will breathe against the neck of a girl
        who knows it
    by the nameless labor.
I am looking for a word to honor those
who left,
inaudible as breath
    inside the talk between us,
as a missing child
        inside the need to breathe.

When the officer comes, give her what she needs.
    Be clear as the pool above the pistol,
        pitiless as the seraphim of noon.
Offer her the voice
        that kneels to make a body small.
There will be time enough to sleep,
    eyes wide as lions of fire.
When a child goes missing, do not pray.
The creatures of your clemency must be known
        to be mysterious.
Be too cold to snow.
There will be weather enough
         to fill your footsteps,
scavengers to eat
       your trail of mercies in the woods.

Most of what I know, I forget.
    But I can tell you where the bodies were,
    how the river bent around them.
    I can tell the story that deepened the voice
            of the officer
        as his eyes glanced away.
Sometimes I lose the names of the innocent.
        But the bodies, I know.
My father told me,
        where books are burned, one day men.
It was raining in Pasadena.
    The scent of avocados floated through screen.
    On a day I forget.
        When I understood so little.

The widow asleep on the table says to the scalpel,
>   *Take of this, my flesh,*
>   as if the knife had a suffering to remove
>   to open up the view.
>   After the guests have left
>   with their kind words and casseroles,
>   the stillness is alive.
>   It is the face in the water at the bottom of a bowl.
>   *You are not alone,*
>   it whispers to the body asleep on the table.
>   *You are asleep on the table.*
>   And just when you thought you understood,
>   the surgeon gets
>   to the quietest part,
>   when he lifts slow the damaged heart
>   and lays the stranger in.

II.

The night custodian takes his earbuds out
    by a wall of glass on the eleventh floor
    to gaze, silent, at the traffic below.
    The song goes on, as strangers
    to their experience do, and the hum
    of the system that blows a chill across the glass.
    The music that makes an hour
        bearable makes the silence music,
but eyes absorb the poison used to clean.
They shed the tears that have no sadness in them.
There will be days a body tells itself,
    first one foot, then another.
To the wounded who remember nothing,
    the past is everywhere
                wounded.

Arvo Pärt is at the piano again,
    staring through the *mirror in the mirror* in the piece
        he plays.
        The ascension of a question,
        the downward movement of reply,
        they make a symmetry so angelic
                he hears in it the stillness
                of the illuminated
                elk.
        He hears a violin
        whose attendant grand piano floats
        uneasy
        through the dome of the cathedral.

If you find paradise disturbing, good.
    If starred
    with animals whose hearts beat fast.

    In every beast, a million
    hydrogen bombs going off at once.
    In the blood
    of the diamond,
            the gore and glory of the sky.

Call him a soul in exile, over and over,
        summoned to write an anthem of return,
    a plainchant
    scored for smoke and scavenger,
    crowned in a wind chime of ice and star.
    On the fulcrum of the A, the lifting of the burden,
    the arc of the cry,
    the sirens of a battered schoolyard.
    If a dead and beautiful language
    opened him up
    one mass grave,
    it was no less personal.
    The sound of one hand talking
            to another,
    the song of the listening
        refugee who sleeps light beneath her god.

I want to ask the deaf in the crowd,
    have you found each other.
    Are you listening with balloons in your hands:
    the Dead passing through.
Do you feel the pulse and courage,
when they play *Morning Dew,*
    and the man
        on lead turn away from the others.
    Can you feel him weep,
    the earth beneath his stack of Twins
    sending waves
    that are long, low, and travel farthest after dark.
    Are gods rearranging the furniture of hell.
    Do they long
                to touch a listener,
        the untouchable center
             in a sphere of air.

In tonight's performance of the late quartet,
    the role of the heroine will be played
    by single strokes of the bow,
    long tones passed
    from cello to viola, viola violin.
    Less about mastery.
    More a winter scene without a story.
    In the graveyards of Saint Petersburg,
        thieves load the marble into carts
      to grind the faces.
When I hear the late chamber music
of Dmitri Shostakovich,
        with its proximity to silence,
I think of this.
What a voice might say,
        if it had the language.
I hear the gentle hiss
    of snow
      falling into eyes
          that do not blink.

The chronicle of dissonance in the new dark age
      will tell you,
   music was never this note.
          Not that one either.
   In a time of plague,
      it was never the crowd
in a tarantella.
It bore no witness, conscience, cure.
If ever it had the nerve to look,
      it had the heart
   to look away.
You could weep for months, years.
        And then, you stop.
     Anything more is madness.
Here in your home on the margins
   beneath the smoke
      of the crematorium,
the moon above the water
        blown to ribbons in the wind.

Grief plurals in the mouths that rise to sing.
    We know, of course,
    one is never the many, the congregate
no body,
    our sacrament no savior.
    We admit and so return
    as animals return at night to the river shore.
        This is my blood.
    So they came,
survivors dressed in orchestra black.
A contralto hung by a thread of music.
    Some felt distracted.
        Others closed their eyes.
There is a sadder, better motherland.
    Some held their faces
in their hands
            to join the music in the dark.

III.

I was a stranger in a strange home
        when the century ended
     and a cloud
of dust chased the people in the street.
A stranger in my cousin's home
when he leaned
his cane against the breakfast table
and watched us
through his inscrutable glass
eye,
the one he earned in Vietnam.

A stranger in Manhattan,
I felt distracted by the shadows that stretched,
    like towers,
       from beautiful women and men,
when an upright piano fell
    from its block and tackle, four floors,
    and the car alarms howled,
    the traffic froze,
each in a net of light across the concrete,
    trapped and speechless,
        waiting for the body to return.

I have had that dream that has no face,
    no mirror to dip my features through.
    If you wake to a wavering curtain,
    the stillness of the air,
        no matter.
Everything comes of nothing, once.
       I have had that mother
         who calls in the middle of the night.
If only fear would grind this tooth into a pill
    and swallow.
The wind is blowing so hard far away in Pasadena,
    I hear it.
I have seen that wind blow a roof into cinders.
Take the medicine, I say.
         Take it, please.
I have raised love's burden far too often
    and never enough.
    I have lifted it,
        hook and mirror,
            to the air.

Let me tell you a story.
    What I recall is the tone,
    when love was a library, small as a toy.
And when she left the room,
there was a door
to a stronger darkness in the dark.
    And slowly it opened. Or closed.
How would I know.
What I remember was the harp
      that kept the stars in place,
   and the air went cold.
What I recall was another child's happiness.
    I loved that child.
    The pins
        that fell from the face of night.
    And what ascended
               was a voice.

When you hear, *Be perfect as your god,*
    can you recall
    your nightmare in the morning.
    Do you hear a piano
    thump ever so gently
    all the notes at once
              in homage.
To what,
     the music never says.
But you smell the burning hair.
The rumored abandonment
just might be yours alone.
It is your nightmare after all.
Your child in a city she has never seen before.
Her home on fire
             because it is holy.

A child returns to her childhood
              as blue does to an infant sky.
   Always more to nightmare that is new.
        I cannot tell you
which rock came from which child
              in the storm of rocks.
           In war, you find
parts impaled on sticks
              at the entrance of the village.
I have worn that look,
          the missing part.
I deserved it.
I don't know why.
       A face so blue it enters paradise
unseen.

The instruments of paradise know no peace
    without it, the *devil's tone*,
    the hook among angelfish,
    so many demons to forgive,
    human hearts to crush into wine,
    a little of the dissonance fades
    the second time you play it,
    and you do.
    Too soon a child is not a child anymore.
    The pictures on her phone bear witness.
    Which is why dissonance is precious
    and needs to be
    preserved. It is the danger music
    come to coax the cage door open,
    the sting of the ecstatic lemon,
    the salt that wakes the boxer,
    the black in the eye that takes
            the last few drops of darkness in.

    Earth consumes a sister,
and those who gather put aside their desire
       to be noticed.
       They talk more softly now,
       as if someone were sleeping
            just over the threshold,
       someone they talk to still
       with the frightened conscience of a child.

So much loneliness is the pretext of fable,
        tell me.
                Does charity need us
to suffer the confusion of stars
                before we pin our gods to them.

Star, as silent as hungry grace, I am talking to you.
        Hard to know
                what a prisoner believes,
    what the guard presumes.

When I first learned of the death of millions,
        I tried to name
        the drowned constellations,
    to make them legible
    and still.

We were all alone with the world back then.

I looked up at my family at the table,
                heads bowed
    to a river

        in the mountains

        in the woods.

IV.

The black cord your car runs over rings a bell,
and you cut the engine and wait, until it dawns:
you could be here all night,
                and no one would notice.
No one would see you stare at the empty office
    with the pale relief
of one whose diagnosis turns suddenly less serious.
For the doctors have shown you the place in the x-ray
    where you live,
      the ghost in the sternum lit
            to keep the thieves away.

Flowers for the tomb, flowers for the lyric soprano,
    flowers for the parlor
        with its portrait
            of flowers.
I hate to leave and say so on pianos
that bear a shock of flowers every spring.
I hate the prayers
in tongues foreign to the flesh
    they pray for,
        mouths stuffed with flowers.
He is with his god,
    says the priest about a friend
        who had no god.
Dust blossoms and falls,
hours, months, years, it falls.
    When a flower fades, it bows.
Over earth, we say, meaning one
        small portion.
One scent behind the petals.
One snow path
    of the bridal gown.

I never met a painting I found *sincere,*
           until I met Saturn,
     eating his child.
And I remembered what my mother said.
To know another's suffering takes a little
    of the madness
       that threatens to consume them.
A nightmare, after all, is a beneficent creature.
The tapes that let me sleep are mostly rain.
Some of them hymns
     that drink the smoke of candles.
No doubt
the painting of Saturn brought the painter
compensation, if not calm.
    To see the terror, there, reunited
with its flesh and problems.
My mother who gave me words
     gave me an unquiet mind.
I never knew where mine ended, hers began.
    I never saw a woman die.
    But here we are,
my mother and I, staring into the same earth
    and garden path,
        until the stones turn blue.

I touched the diamonds of the untouched canvas,
    the extremities of blue
            in the long unruly hair of trees,
  a portrait of a man as a mountain.
I tell the animals who sleep with me.
They do not speak,
but still I feel persuaded to confide.
Once, I heard a mountain whisper.
I am so tired of hating myself, loving myself,
  and who is not,
    who can tell the one from the other.
I could have stood there for an hour.
I could have wept and awakened,
    never the wiser.
          I was a survivor after all.

When I first saw the ditches of Görlitz,
               the caption read: *remember.*
Overhead,
    an *abyss of birds* scored for clarinet,
prisoner, cello, whatever history could provide.
When you hear it,
you see the world through the diamonds
                 of a chain-link fence.
Merciful and cruel,
    the distant boughs of the Black Forest.
    Is this, I wondered,
what a dead man wants,
               what a prisoner heard.
The abyss of unappeasable beauty in the world.

V.

I used to seek the company of a friend
    who sat across the table and, in silence, read.
    He would drink all night,
    but days were ours,
        and sometimes we looked up
    and talked of something we found funny or wise.
    It seemed like nothing then,
        let alone—
        days
        his body
        lay, undiscovered—
            the quiet mercy
        that it is.

The body, we know, is mostly water,
    like money and medications and marriage
    in Los Angeles.
The truth is not the truth,
        says a lawyer for a president,
but if you look close,
you can see a foreign object in his eye.
Breath too is mostly water,
    like modern life
        in the eyes of creatures
who do not love you, and the uncle
who did,
who penned a letter and walked into the great Pacific.
Ashes to ashes, we say.
    But the body is mostly water.
It is what we do not speak about,
    as men so rarely speak of the love
    between them,
        pouring through the mountain in the rain.

Not this face,
        the broken mineshaft of the eyes,
        the pallor of the mask,
        but the radiance of blood on which it floats.
        I find my sacrament there.
        When a friend dies, I see her everywhere.
        Every step a step in the lifeboat.
        The boy who pours my coffee sways
        to a music in his head,
        and the crumpling of the stream
        turns the color of a letter I did not send:
        I am sorry, it says.
                For what, I do not know.
        Perhaps it is death
                that speaks on my behalf.
        The crippling of the bridge between us.
            The sound of fire
                laid in the water.

River consumes river, the water the shore.
    We learned it as children.
    But the length of a life never comes.
        Is that what people call a death rattle,
    I asked.
    And the nurse made a crucifix
with the axis
of her finger on her lips.
I felt small.
Like a pin that holds the wheel of a toy.
So when it was over, I had a child's face.
I stood before an ocean
                as motionless as stone.
    If only I were that still,
                I could walk across.
    I could step out of the picture
                and never make a wave.

I am sending off my blood
    for the story of who I am
        —I am only human after all—
and a stranger writes me back.
    He says, I knew a woman
        who touched herself, endlessly,
    to tell her body she was there.
The bruises vanished long ago.
All that was left was nerves.
    Not enlightenment.
        Not the others in the room.
    Not the blackboard equation
wiped down to starless paradise below.
When a mind leaves a body, it leaves
a figure in the snow
        and drifts deeper into refuge.
If you travel north far enough,
you will find her.
You will walk an Earth
that is not Earth anymore.
    It is a terrified sea
        of diamonds.
    Every fear is a fear of nothing.

The drone of a train in the distance,
  the roar of the trash bin
    wheeled across a street,
  the cry of a cat
  or is it a child,
all that chance has given you at dawn,
play back the tape one day,
  when you are older,
forgetting why you made it.
Everywhere the unspeakable
surplus,
the sound of rain
in a rustle of leaves.
You have the kind of friend that is never true
  or untrue,
    but vital and unconscious,
as oceans are.
The accidental music says,
take heart,
the world was here before you
    and will be here long after,
though you know better.
Dear friend, dear Earth,
dear last few hours of lamplight
  on the shore.

The plural of music keeps changing
    back to *music*.
In paradise, everyone is powerless.
The smoke of a locomotive
lies down
in a grave of air.
          From the lip of iron,
              the whiteness of the ash.
In a crowded room,
        I hear the sound of *no one*
above the laughter of the others.
I tell myself. I will remember.
        I will see the train,
the chafing of its breath,
the *chalk, chalk* of some dark progress.
           The gaze of a girl,
    her mother's lip,
                I see it,
   the parting there
             where the song begins.

Wherever I go, no one is there.
    Fog moans, roils, burns.
    A river ends in a vast amnesia
    of waves.
    No one here to mourn the mother.
    No memorial, she said.
No seagull floats across a mountain in the dark.
    No cigarette between strangers
    beneath a bridge called *suicide*,
        because that gave it power.
        No one is here,
        we say,
        when we are there to see it.
    Wherever I go,
    a girl laid in a river.
    A siren wailed in the distance like a cradle.
      Down the cleft of the sluice,
            strung
      with hair,
    the chill of water
        passing through us all.

NOTES

1   Václav Cílek quotation is from *To Breathe with Birds* (2015).

59   George Santayana quotation is from *Winds of Doctrine* (1913).

117 Samuel Beckett quotation is from *Company* (1975).

www.ingramcontent.com/pod-product-compliance
Lightning Source LLC
Chambersburg PA
CBHW031454160426
43195CB00010BB/977